THE TABERNACLE

THE TABERNACLE

THE PLAN OF THE TABERNACLE

```
┌──────────────────────────────────────────────────────────┐
│                                                            │
│   ┌─────────────────────┐                                  │
│   │ Holy of  │  ┌─┐ D    │                                 │
│50 │ Holies   │  └─┘      │    ┌───┐      ┌─────┐           │
│Cub│   ┌─┐    │ ┌─┐Holy   │    │ B │      │     │           │
│its│   └─┘    │ └─┘Place  │    │   │      │  A  │           │
│   │ F        │ E ┌─┐ C   │    └───┘      └─────┘           │
│   │          │   └─┘     │                                 │
│   └─────────────────────┘                                  │
│         30 Cubits                                          │
│                                          Courtyard         │
│                                                            │
└──────────────────────────────────────────────────────────┘
                        100 Cubits
```

A - Brazen Altar   B - Laver   C - Lampstand   D - Table
E - Altar of Incense   F - Ark of the Covenant

Key Points

- The Tabernacle was God's dwelling place during Israel's time in the wilderness and once they reached the Promised Land.
- Its structure and materials were designed to teach the Israelites lessons about their God.
- The Tabernacle was designed and built according to a divine plan.
- The New Testament writers use the Tabernacle to illustrate spiritual truths such as the humanity of Christ and His atoning death.

The Institution

In Eden God visited Adam and Eve. He came down in the "cool of the day" (Gen. 3:8) and "walked"[1] there. This indicates that God's personal presence was not a permanent feature of Eden. It also indicates that when He did come down He was approachable. Since He moved at walking pace, Adam could approach Him and walk with Him. It may also convey the idea that He came to enjoy His creation as well as the company of man. Once the Fall occurred He withdrew Himself and spoke to man from heaven (Gen. 6:13; 7:1; 12:1) and occasionally appeared in visions (Gen. 15:1; 17:1) and in other ways e.g. the bush

---

[1] God did not literally "walk" since God is a spirit and does not have legs and feet. This is what is called an anthropomorphism i.e. attributing to God human characteristics. Elsewhere in scripture God is said to have "eyes", "ears", an "arm" and a "hand".

which burned but was not consumed (Ex. 3:2).[2] But after choosing Israel to be His people from all the peoples of the earth, God decided that He would not only redeem them and lead them to Canaan but also live with them (Ex. 25:22; 29:43). Exodus describes the day when He came to dwell among His people (Ex. 40:34). The Tabernacle remained the dwelling place of God until the Temple was completed. Thereafter Jehovah dwelt in the temple. Scripture does not make it clear whether the glory, as a symbol of His presence, remained in the tabernacle and temple permanently. At one point the ark was removed from the tabernacle when captured by the Philistines and there is no indication of the glory following the ark. Likewise during the history of the divided Kingdoms some of Judah's kings let the temple go to rack and ruin. It must be doubted whether God's glory remained in that circumstance. When Ezekiel was in exile in Babylon he saw a vision of the glory leaving the temple in Jerusalem (Ezek. 10:19; 11:23). This was in anticipation of the destruction of the temple in about 587BC (2 Kings 25:2-7; 2 Chron. 36:18-21). It also marked God's displeasure with the idolatrous practises that were occurring there. The period between the descent of the glory in Sinai and its departure in Ezekiel's vision is about 1000 years.

The Interpretation
The word "tabernacle" means a dwelling place and can be used to refer to an ordinary dwelling. But "the Tabernacle" in the O.T. usually refers to a specific dwelling place namely the dwelling place of God. Sometimes it is simply called the "tent" to indicate that it was not a permanent structure. Another common name is the "Tabernacle of the Congregation" or, more accurately, "Tent of Meeting". Sometimes it is called the "Tent of the Testimony" (e.g. Num. 9:15) or the "House of the Lord" (e.g. Ex. 23:19) or the "Tabernacle of the Lord" (1 Kings 2:28). These names all emphasise different aspects of the Tabernacle. It was the place where the Israelites "met" God. It was the place where the "testimony" (the two tables of the law) was stored and its centrality acknowledged. It was the place where the "Lord" made His "house" in the midst of His people.

The Implementation
Moses, a Levite, entrusted the task of construction to Bezaleel and Aholiab, from the tribes of Judah and Dan. The plan was shown to Moses by God on Mount Sinai with the instruction that it was to be meticulously implemented.

---

[2] Sometimes called theophanies (from *"theos"* – God and *"phaino"* – to appear) or where it is a pre-incarnate appearance of Christ, Christophanies.

The record of scripture probably does not repeat everything Moses saw in the vision he was given. Though scripture does not tell us everything e.g. the details about the dimensions and appearance of the laver are skimpy and information about the appearance of the cherubim is limited, it is evident that Moses had been shown and had seen all that was required to build the Tabernacle. The materials were supplied by the people. There was considerable sacrifice involved in the preparation of materials for the construction. Women donated their gold jewellery and brass looking glasses. The wood was cut from shittim or acacia trees growing in the wilderness. The skins which covered the tent may have been owned by the Israelites or acquired by trading with nomadic peoples in the Wilderness. The "badger" skin mentioned in the A.V. was either ram skin or the skins of a sea creature called a "sea cow". Some think dolphin skin was used. The Israelites were close to the sea for most of their journey to Sinai so this is a possibility. Considerable artistic and mechanical skills were used in spinning the blue, purple and scarlet yarn, weaving the white linen and beating and casting the various vessels and implements out of gold, silver and brass (or copper).

The Interior
Strictly speaking the word Tabernacle is distinct from the courtyard that surrounded it. The Tabernacle itself was the tent in the courtyard. It was divided into two compartments, the first (the Holy Place) somewhat larger than the second (the Holy of Holies). If we may speak of God having a location in the Universe, that location during the existence of the Tabernacle/Temple was above the Mercy Seat and between the wings of the cherubim inside the Holy of Holies. His presence was signified by a cloud of glory that shone above the Ark. In addition there was a pillar that appeared above the Tabernacle. By day it had the appearance of a pillar of smoke and at night a pillar of fire (Num. 9:15 and 16).

The Inauguration
The Tabernacle was constructed over a period of about 6 months by the nation of Israel. They took 3 months to get to Sinai (Ex. 19:1). Moses ascended and descended the Mount on a number of occasions before the ascent of 40 days' duration when he received the vision of the Tabernacle. We know that they dedicated the Tabernacle on the anniversary of their departure from Egypt (Ex. 40:17). It must have taken about 6 months to construct and assemble. The Israelites carried the Tabernacle with them through their 40 years in the

Wilderness. After they conquered Canaan the Israelites entered the Land. Since the Tabernacle was designed to be a structure which could be moved many of its features became redundant. Until it was replaced by a permanent structure, the temple, the Tabernacle was based at a number of locations.[3] There is a hint that the altar was removed and placed elsewhere and it is certainly the case that the Ark was removed. Its final resting place was Jerusalem.

The Interruption

When Solomon built the temple (about 959 BC) the need for the Tabernacle ceased. Some of its vessels were replaced e.g. a new altar was constructed on a far larger scale, a new laver was built and called a "Sea", probably because of the vast quantity of water it held (1 Kings 7:23). The Ark remained and was placed with its staves in the new Holy of Holies. The Temple was eventually destroyed by the Babylonians and the vessels removed (2 Chron. 36:18) in about 587 BC. It is probable that the Ark was removed to Babylon at this time. What became of it is unknown. The Temple was after the return from captivity rebuilt with new vessels and furniture (about 516 BC). But this new temple (refurbished and expanded by Herod) was also destroyed by the Romans in 70 AD. There is a relief of the triumphal procession of the Roman Emperor Titus in Rome which shows what appears to be the candlestick being taken into Rome after the Romans captured Jerusalem and destroyed the temple in 70 AD.

It would seem however that this present period or interval of time will end and that the tabernacle will one day again be with men (Rev. 21:3). In the Millennium there will be a temple (Ezek. 40 et seq.) and in the Eternal State God will have His tabernacle or dwelling place with men.

The present whereabouts of the Ark of the Covenant remains a source of fascination. Some have speculated that it was not destroyed by the Babylonians or Romans but is hidden in a chamber under the site of the old temple. "Indiana Jones and the Raiders of the Lost Ark" a Hollywood film is built on the notion that the ark was found and taken into the custody of the US Government![4]

---

[3] Shiloh – Josh 18:1; Nob – 1 Sam 21:1 et seq. Gibeon – 1 Chron 21:29; 2 Chron 1:3; David made ready a tent in Jerusalem (1 Chron. 15:1) before the Tabernacle's furniture was moved there. Of the furniture, only the Ark seems to have survived the cessation of the Tabernacle as an institution.
[4] "Raiders of the Lost Ark".

Its Importance

The Tabernacle may no longer exist but its furniture and construction remain important for Christians today. It is an important "visual aid" for Christians. It illustrates aspects of the deity and humanity of the Lord Jesus. John in his Gospel nods in this direction when he states that He "tabernacled among us" (Jn. 1:14 *lit.*). In the N.T. the human body is often depicted as a tent. But in John chapter 1 it is evident that it is designed to remind us of the glory within the Tabernacle as well as the plain exterior skins. The author of Hebrews uses its various compartments to depict the relationship of earth to heaven. The Holy of Holies is God's immediate presence (Heb. 8:2 - "the true tabernacle"; 9:11 - "a greater and more perfect tabernacle"; 9:12 - "the holy place"). To enter there as a High Priest the Lord Jesus passed into heaven. In other words attention is drawn to His movement through the court and Holy Place. In ch 10:19 His flesh is the veil which was the means of entrance into heaven. The mercy seat is a picture in Romans 3:25 of the Lord Jesus and His death.

 **KEY SCRIPTURES**

⁸ And let them make me a sanctuary; that I may dwell among them. ⁹ According to all that I shew thee, *after* the pattern of the tabernacle, and the pattern of all the instruments thereof, even so shall ye make *it.*

Ex. 25:8-9

³⁴ Then a cloud covered the tent of the congregation, and the glory of the LORD filled the tabernacle. ³⁵ And Moses was not able to enter into the tent of the congregation, because the cloud abode thereon, and the glory of the LORD filled the tabernacle. ³⁶ And when the cloud was taken up from over the tabernacle, the children of Israel went onward in all their journeys: ³⁷ But if the cloud were not taken up, then they journeyed not till the day that it was taken up. ³⁸ For the cloud of the LORD was upon the tabernacle by day, and fire was on it by night, in the sight of all the house of Israel, throughout all their journeys.

Ex. 40:34-38

²⁴ being justified freely by his grace through the redemption which *is* in Christ Jesus; ²⁵ whom God has set forth a mercy-seat, through faith in his blood, for *the* shewing forth of his righteousness, in respect of the passing by the sins that had taken place before, through the forbearance of God;

Rom. 3:24-25 (J.N.D.)

¹⁴ And the Word was made flesh, and dwelt (*skenoo* - pitched his tent) among us, (and we beheld his glory, the glory as of the only begotten of the Father,) full of grace and truth.

Jn. 1:14

¹⁹ Having therefore, brethren, boldness to enter into the holiest by the blood of Jesus, ²⁰ By a new and living way, which he hath consecrated for us, through the veil, that is to say, his flesh;

Heb. 10:19-20

The details of the tabernacle were given around 1500 years before Christ and they are full of His glory. It becomes most interesting and indeed soul thrilling to observe that the type is fulfilled in the antitype... nothing... was left to the imagination or discretion of Moses. Numerous times in Exodus Moses was commanded to see that the tabernacle was made according to the pattern that God showed him on the Mount.

Albert Leckie

The Tabernacle is of such importance to God's redemptive programme that 50 chapters in the Bible are given to explaining its pattern, construction and service. Nothing was left to Moses' speculation; God revealed to him in minute detail every aspect of the Tabernacle. More than 20 times we read "as the Lord commanded Moses"... for almost 500 years the Tabernacle served as a place for God to dwell among His people.... The Tabernacle stood as a visual reminder to Israel that they served the true and living God. It helped keep Israel from idol worship that was practised by those living around them as they made their pilgrimage through the wilderness.[6]

David Levy

---

[6] The Tabernacle. Shadows of the Messiah p.16.

KEY QUESTIONS

1. In what sense did God "live" in the Tabernacle?

2. What other names was the Tabernacle known by?

3. Why did Israel cease to use the Tabernacle?

4. Which New Testament passages refer to the Tabernacle and for what purposes?

The Altar

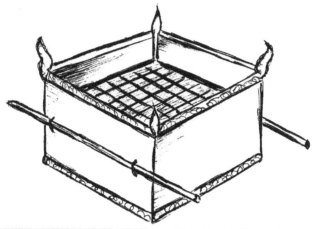

Key Points

- The altar was the place where sacrifices were burnt and presented to God.

- It was the first vessel in the Tabernacle courtyard indicating that sin must be put away before God can be approached.

- The brass used in the altar typifies God's judgement.

- The altar speaks of the death of Christ, the ultimate sacrifice for sin.

The Altar's Function

Sometimes called the Altar of Burnt Offering or the Brazen (i.e. brass) Altar, to distinguish it from the Golden Altar, it was the largest, though probably not the heaviest, item in the Tabernacle and stood inside the entrance of the Tabernacle (Ex. 40:29). Altars[7] in scripture were a type of platform on which the carcasses of dead animals were placed after being killed. The bodies of the animals were then laid on wood which had been placed on the altar. Once in the flames the bodies were burnt and turned into ashes and smoke. The smoke produced by the body rose upwards. This symbolised the idea that they were offered to

---

[7] Heb. *mizbē* – "place of slaughter or sacrifice".

God who dwelt above in heaven. The remainder was reduced to ash. The altar in the Tabernacle had a grate. The ash fell through the grate and was periodically removed by the priest. The ashes were regarded as sacred and were disposed of carefully (Lev. 4:12, 6:10-11).

The Altar's Form

The Altar of the Tabernacle was more sophisticated than the impromptu altars that had been used hitherto by the Patriarchs. It was made of brass,[8] a precious metal. This reflected its status. Brass is also repeatedly connected in scripture with God's judgement ("serpent of brass" – Num. 21:9; "heavens as brass" – Deut. 28:23[9]; "Feet like brass" - Rev. 1:15[10]). It also has associations with strength (Job 6:12; 41:27). The horns that decorated the four corners of the altar symbolise the idea of strength. Bulls and rams and other animals had horns and used them to defend themselves or attack enemies. The horn became a symbol of power in Israel. Some have also suggested they were used to tether animals which had been brought to the altar.[11] The Altar's design assisted the consummation of the sacrifice. The grate was inserted into the altar half way up its side and air passing through it provided an draught which supplied the flames which burnt the sacrifice which lay on the grate above.

The altar was not just made of brass. It was also made of wood. The shittim or acacia wood, which was used throughout the Tabernacle, was sheathed in metal. It appears to have been beaten into sheets and attached to the wood with nails or pins. Why the wood did not char because of the heat of the flames and the conducting qualities of the brass is the subject of intense discussion. If the underlying wood could have charred the serviceability of the altar would have been seriously impaired. Bronze has very low conductivity and brass slightly more so. Copper conducts at similar levels to gold and silver. Whatever the position the design must have protected the wood.

---

[8] It is not certain what "brass" was. It may have been what we call copper. It may have been bronze. Copper and bronze are alloys.
[9] This may indicate that the colour of the sky was copper in colour because of sandstorms or that the sky was hard like copper and gave no rain. Either way it signified God's judgement during drought conditions. Cf. Lev. 26:19 – imagery reversed.
[10] The primary reference here is perhaps to the colour of brass or copper when it is molten. It exudes heat and light. Since the Lord Jesus is depicted as the Judge who is coming to exact vengeance, the link with brass is obvious (see Ezek. 40:3).
[11] Psalm 118:27.

The Altar was portable. It had rings attached to its extremities. Staves or poles could be run through the rings and it could then be carried when the Israelites struck camp and moved on through the Wilderness.

Although there is no mention of it, some have thought that in order to hoist the carcasses of animals or the parts of the butchered carcass on to the altar, there must have been some form of ramp. There is a general prohibition on steps (cf. Ex. 20:26) at altars so that the priest's leg or ankle would not be visible as he mounted the steps. One might think that a ramp would give rise to the same risk. The ledge around the altar may have assisted the lifting of animals on to the altar as would the tools provided for the altar. The fleshhooks were large forks with which the carcasses of large animals could be moved by the priests when out of reach. Whether the massive altars of Solomon's temple or Ezekiel's temple necessitated ramps is another matter.

The Altar's Foreshadowings

The altar meant nothing without a sacrifice and the sacrifice meant nothing without a worshipper moved by faith in God (Ps. 51:16, 17). Sacrifice taught the Israelites that although God cared for them and protected them, a relationship with Him depended on their sin being forgiven. Sin could not be dealt with by anything other than death. While strictly their sin involved the forfeiture of their own lives, God permitted animals to die as their substitute. The Altar was the place where the substitute was offered. The Altar anticipated Calvary where the Lord Jesus offered Himself as the final substitute for sin.

The Israelites did not have free passage in the Tabernacle. They could enter the Tabernacle courtyard by the gate and stand by the Altar but could go no further. The priests alone were permitted to go into the Tabernacle itself. The position of the Altar at the entrance was an important lesson that sacrifice for sin was necessary for anyone who wished to draw near to God. Since the priests were permitted to take meat from the offerings, it was also a source of food for the priesthood.

 **KEY SCRIPTURES**

¹ And thou shalt make an altar *of* shittim wood, five cubits long, and five cubits broad; the altar *shall be* foursquare: and the height thereof shall be three cubits. ² And thou shalt make the horns of it upon the four corners thereof: his horns shall be of the same: and thou shalt overlay it with brass. ³ And thou shalt make his pans to receive his ashes, and his shovels, and his basons, and his fleshhooks, and his firepans: all the vessels thereof thou shalt make *of* brass. ⁴ And thou shalt make for it a grate of network *of* brass; and upon the net shalt thou make four brasen rings in the four corners thereof. ⁵ And thou shalt put it under the compass of the altar beneath, that the net may be even to the midst of the altar. ⁶ And thou shalt make staves for the altar, staves *of* shittim wood, and overlay them with brass. ⁷ And the staves shall be put into the rings, and the staves shall be upon the two sides of the altar, to bear it. ⁸ Hollow with boards shalt thou make it: as it was shewed thee in the mount, so shall they make *it*.

Ex. 27:1-8

¹⁰ We have an altar, whereof they have no right to eat which serve the tabernacle.

Heb. 13:10

KEY QUOTES

The Brazen altar was the basis of the Levitical system. To it the sinner came with his Divinely appointed victim. There was a fire continually burning upon it (Lev. 6:13), and the daily sacrifice was renewed each morning. There it stood: ever smoking, ever blood-stained, ever open to any guilty Hebrew that might wish to approach it. The sinner, having forfeited his life by sin, another life—an innocent one—must be given in his stead. When the Israelite brought his offering, before killing it he laid his hand on the animal's head, thus becoming identified with it, and thereby the acceptableness of the flawless victim passed to him, while his sin is transferred to it. So, too, this Altar stood in the path of the priests, as they went in to minister within the Holy Place.[12]

Arthur Pink

The altar was made of shittim wood, termed in the Septuagint... "incorruptible wood" thus pointing to the incorruptible humanity of our Lord, but the wood was overlaid with brass, the only metal which could withstand fire; so in this we witness the divine ability of Christ to endure the fierce and unrelenting fire of judgement.[13]

Walter Scott

---

[12] Gleanings in Exodus p.242.
[13] The Tabernacle: Its Structure and Symbolism (Ambassador Publications) p.44.

KEY QUESTIONS

1. What were the two materials with which the altar was built and what did they signify?

2. What was the purpose of the horns on the altar?

3. What happened with the ashes that were left behind after the sacrifice?

4. Should we still use altars?

The Laver

Key Points

- The Laver was the vessel the priests used to wash their hands and feet when serving in the Tabernacle.

- Like the Altar the Laver was made of brass or bronze indicating that it typified the removal of sin.

- The Laver was filled with water. Still water in scripture is associated with the Word of God.

The Laver's Function

The Laver is a Hebrew word (*kiyor*) which means "basin". The translators of the A.V. translated the word as "laver" since a laver is a bowl or basin used for washing. That was the function of this vessel. It enabled the priests to wash their hands and feet. This was both a practical necessity as well as symbolic act. Priests had to sacrifice animals and divide the carcass. This was messy work. They also had to remove the ashes that gathered beneath the Altar. Hence the need to wash is obvious. Every morning and evening one of the priests had to offer a sacrifice (Ex. 29:38). Thereafter he had to enter the Holy Place to tend the lamps or offer incense (Ex. 30:7, 8). It would not have been appropriate for him to do so with his hands still stained with blood or dusty from the ash from the altar.   But the symbolism of cleansing is also important. Even if the priest's hands were clean he would still clean his hands as a symbolic acknowledgement of his impurity before God. The laver must have been in constant use in the Wilderness. At that time the priesthood was composed of three men. They would constantly be engaged in the work of sacrifice and in constant need of the laver.[14]

The Laver's Form

There is little detail given about the construction or size of the Laver.[15]   It was designed to contain water and so must have been a receptacle of some sort. It probably was shaped like a bowl. Because the priests had to wash their feet as well as hands some have thought there was a lower bowl for the feet and an upper bowl for the hands but there is no direct evidence for this.   The fact that they washed their feet does not necessitate two bowls. Water could have been scooped out and applied to the priests' feet or decanted into a bowl or cup and used for washing. Whatever its design it was based on a pedestal called the "foot". Like the altar of burnt offering the laver was made of brass. The laver is the only vessel that came from a single source. We are told that the women who assembled at the door of the Tabernacle (Ex. 38:8) donated their looking glasses to make the Laver. No doubt there were other items that were made of brass but the Laver was made only of looking glasses. It is reasonable to assume that there must have been quite a number of looking glasses if they were sufficient to provide metal for the Laver from them. Looking glasses may be for the benign purpose of keeping neat and tidy but they may also foster an unhealthy interest in appearances. When they were donated to Moses they became devoted to sacred purposes. Instead of indulging vanity they were used to maintain the purity of the priests.

It was positioned between the altar and the entrance to the Tabernacle (Ex. 40:7). This was exactly where it needed to be since the priest who moved from the altar to the Tabernacle needed to be clean. The laver is not one of the vessels

---

[14] Nadab and Abihu perished after offering "strange fire". This may have involved offering incense in censers in a way contrary to the command of God or it may have been a reference to offering while under the influence of alcohol and thus in a way inconsistent with God's holiness – Lev. 10:1,2,8.

[15] The great "sea" and the ten lavers of Solomon's Temple are described in greater detail in 1 Kings 7:23-39; 2 Chron. 4:1-10.

mentioned in Numbers 4 which had to be covered in transit. The absence of
rings and poles suggest that it was not large or heavy.

The Laver's Foreshadowings
If the Altar taught that sin must be put away by sacrifice, the laver taught that
those that approach God must be clean. When a priest entered the priesthood
his whole body was washed (Ex. 29:4; Lev. 8:6). The Law did not require that
washing to be repeated. By contrast the cleansing of the laver was a constant
necessity. This indicates that the Laver is not symbolic of initial sanctification
which is a "once for all" thing (e.g. 1 Cor. 6:11; Eph. 5:26). It is symbolic of the on-
going work of sanctification (e.g. 2 Cor. 7:1).

The Lord's teaching in the Upper Room illustrates this. The Lord in an act of
humility offered to wash the disciples' feet. When Peter refused to permit the
Lord to wash his feet, the Lord insisted. He drew a parallel between what He
offered to do physically with what He could do spiritually. To refuse to be washed[16]
by Christ (Jn. 13:8) was akin to refusing to wash in the Laver. If the priest did not
wash at the Laver he would not have been permitted to draw near to God in the
Holy Place which would hinder his service, though he would still be a priest. The
Lord Jesus then spoke of another washing (Jn 13:10) which involved complete
cleansing.[17] The Lord taught Peter that if he had not been bathed he would be
in the same position as Judas, an unbeliever. This parallels the all over cleansing
that the priest received when he entered the priesthood (cf. Heb. 10:22). These
truths are also taught by John in his epistles (1 John 1:9).

In scripture water is a symbol of a variety of truths. Speaking generally water
is of two sorts. There is "living" water. This is water that moves and is full of
energy. It may be water that rushes upwards like the spring, or water that flows
onwards like the river or water that falls down, like the rain. Usually this type of
water is a symbol of the regenerating work of God often through the Holy Spirit
(Is. 44:3-5; Jn. 4:14; 7:38; Rev. 21:6; 22:17). Water that is enclosed in a pool or
vessel has different characteristics. It is limpid and still. This type of water is
often symbolic of God's spoken (Jn 15:3; Eph. 5:25-26) or written word (Ps 119:9).
Water in a vessel is still water but is more frequently associated with cleansing
and refreshment than flowing water.

[16] Nipso.
[17] Leloumenos.

James likens scripture to a mirror, very like the looking glasses of the women (Jas. 1:23-25). While the looking glass can show us when we are unclean only the laver can enable us to do something about it.

 **KEY SCRIPTURES**

¹⁷ And the LORD spake unto Moses, saying, ¹⁸ Thou shalt also make a laver *of* brass, and his foot *also of* brass, to wash *withal*: and thou shalt put it between the tabernacle of the congregation and the altar, and thou shalt put water therein. ¹⁹ For Aaron and his sons shall wash their hands and their feet thereat: ²⁰ When they go into the tabernacle of the congregation, they shall wash with water, that they die not; or when they come near to the altar to minister, to burn offering made by fire unto the LORD: ²¹ So they shall wash their hands and their feet, that they die not: and it shall be a statute for ever to them, *even* to him and to his seed throughout their generations.

Ex. 30:17-21

⁸ And he made the laver *of* brass, and the foot of it *of* brass, of the looking glasses of *the women* assembling, which assembled *at* the door of the tabernacle of the congregation.

Ex. 38:8

⁴ He riseth from supper, and laid aside his garments; and took a towel, and girded himself. ⁵ After that he poureth water into a bason, and began to wash the disciples' feet, and to wipe *them* with the towel wherewith he was girded. ⁶ Then cometh he to Simon Peter: and Peter saith unto him, Lord, dost thou wash my feet? ⁷ Jesus answered and said unto him, What I do thou knowest not now; but thou shalt know hereafter. ⁸ Peter saith unto him, Thou shalt never wash my feet. Jesus answered him, If I wash thee not, thou hast no part with me. ⁹ Simon Peter saith unto him, Lord, not my feet only, but also *my* hands and *my* head. ¹⁰ Jesus saith to him, He that is washed needeth not save to wash *his* feet, but is clean every whit: and ye are clean, but not all.

Jn. 13:4-10

 **KEY QUOTES**

The laver was placed between the altar and the door and the priests were commanded to wash their hands and feet thereat. It was an easy matter for the once cleansed hands and feet to contract defilement. The hands constantly working in the service of God at the altar and the feet ever walking on the desert sand would be in continuous need of washing, and for this the water in the laver was given.[18]

John Ritchie

It is significant that no measurements are given for the Laver. Why is this? "We are not told that it is so high or so large in circumference... the Altar had measurements which speaks of the claims of the throne, measured and met by Christ. In relation to sin, Christ was the only one who knew exactly how to weigh these claims, and how to satisfy them. But when we come to the Laver we have to do with the claims of God upon His people...where is the one who can say, 'I know the claims of the Word of God and have fully met them' " (WJ McClure).[19]

John Grant

---

[18] The Tabernacle in the Wilderness (John Ritchie) p. 58.
[19] Believers Magazine December 2008.

KEY QUESTIONS

1. Why did the priest need to wash himself?

2. What does still water symbolise in the Bible?

3. Who provided the materials for the Laver?

4. Why was the Laver not made of gold or silver?

The Vessels in the Holy Place

Key Points

- The vessels in the Holy Place were the Golden Altar, the Table of Shewbread and the Lampstand.

- The Table symbolised God's fellowship with Israel.

- The Golden Altar symbolised the prayers of the people to God.

- The Lampstand symbolised the illumination of God through the Spirit.

In contrast to the two bronze vessels in the Outer Court the vessels in the Holy Place were constructed with gold. The Golden Lampstand was made of one solid gold piece and the Table of Shewbread and Altar of Incense of wood overlaid with gold. The vessels in the Outer Court were designed to deal with sin and ceremonial defilement. The vessels within the Holy Place were designed to manifest God and His glory. The vessels in the Holy Place were made of gold to express this change in purpose. Gold is more attractive and costly than bronze.

The Table of Shewbread

The table has a symbolic meaning in scripture. It is the place where people share meals together. It symbolises friendship and fellowship. It speaks of kindness and hospitality. David famously speaks of a table spread by the Lord in Psalm 23 even when he was surrounded by his enemies.[20] In the N.T. the Lord Jesus sat at the same table as "publicans and sinners" (Matt. 9:10). He sat at the table in the home in Bethany (Jn. 12:2) and again with His disciples in the Upper Room before Calvary (Lk. 22:21).

The Table of Shewbread emphasised that the Tabernacle was a place where man could have fellowship with God albeit this fellowship was through the priest. The ordinary man could not approach the Holy Place.

Although the Tabernacle speaks of the Lord and of His Son, the Lord Jesus, we also find in it emblems of creation. The cherubim are represented. The almond flowers and buds represent the botanic creation. The twelve loaves correspond to the twelve tribes. In reality they were characterised by murmuring and idolatry. But the twelve loaves emphasised what they should be. They were made of fine wheat (Lev. 24:5). Josephus[21] states that they were unleavened. Frankincense was sprinkled on the loaves. They were renewed every week so they remained fresh. The fine wheat speaks of consistency of character, the absence of leaven speaks of holiness and the frankincense of that which is sweet and attractive to God. God could "feed" on that which was pure, holy and sweet. All of this was of course seen perfectly in Christ, the ideal Israelite.

---

[20] The altar is described at times as a "table" (Mal. 1:7; Ezek. 44:16). This may suggest that the offerings provided that upon which God "fed" (Lev. 21:6) and which in turn provided food for the priests.
[21] Antiquities of the Jews Book 3 ch 6 para. 6.

Each loaf was 2/10 of an unspecified measure of flour. If (as many translations assume) it was 2/10 of an ephah of flour[22] this is a substantial amount of flour and would mean that these were large loaves. Given the dimensions of the table it would be difficult to accommodate twelve large loaves in two rows of six. But if it was 2/10 of a smaller measure then the problem is removed. If the loaves were large then they might have been stacked. Some think that the word "row"[23] in the A.V. should be translated "pile". But it is hard to believe the loaves were in piles since the table would be difficult to transport without the loaves spilling over the edge of the table![24]

Every week the priests were permitted to remove and eat the shewbread (Lev. 24:9). So the loaves represent not only what the Lord delights in and "feeds" upon but it is also what we should feed on. If we are to see bread in the Tabernacle as a depiction of Christ it is best seen in the manna deposited in the golden pot. The "bread from heaven" (Ex. 16:33; Jn. 6:31) was a type of Christ.

The Golden Lampstand
Although the A.V. refers to this vessel as the candlestick it is perhaps better to speak of it as the Lampstand since there was no wax used in it. It gave light from seven lamps fed by olive oil each with a wick. The Lampstand[25] was a highly ornate vessel and evidently meant to be beautiful. Almond flowers and buds were carved or beaten into the gold. The cups into which the oil was poured seem to have been upturned bowls carved to look like petals. The bible does not give any indication of its size or dimensions. The Lampstand stood (Ex. 26:35) on the south side of the Holy Place, to the priest's left as he faced the Ark.

Apart from the Lampstand there would have been no light for the priest as he offered incense or handled the bread. The outer veil cut off the natural light. The seven lamps ensured that there was adequate light to work with. The golden boards that lined the Tabernacle must have reflected the light of the Lampstand and made it a beautiful place in which to work.

---

[22] An ephah is about 7 pounds or $3^1/_4$ kilograms.
[23] Heb. *ārak* - lit. "to set or arrange in order".
[24] Num. 4:7 states that the bread was kept on the table during transport.
[25] Heb. *menorah*.

The Lampstand had one central stem and six branches so that there were seven lamps in total. Seven is perhaps the most important number in scripture. It is linked with the idea of completion or perfection. There are seven days in a week and the seventh day the Sabbath was the day God completed His work. The seven Feasts of Jehovah (Lev. 23) cover the whole religious cycle of a year. The seven churches of Asia (Rev. 2-3) represent the whole cycle of church testimony. The Lampstand therefore represents perfect illumination. The flame was supplied by oil. The oil sat in little cups and in the oil was a wick which required to be lit and trimmed by the priests. The oil was produced by beating olives and catching the oil it produced. It had to be pure oil, free of any impurities. Oil in scripture was used as fuel for lamps, in baking or cooking, its soothing properties made it suitable for medicinal purposes (Lk. 10:34; Mk 6:13), it was used to soften and enhance skin (Psalm 104:15) and for other cosmetic purposes. It was used symbolically to mark the appointment of kings and prophets. The word "anoint" (*māšah*) means to pour or smear oil on a person or object. The Messiah (*māšîah*) is the anointed one.

The light was fed with pure oil. Oil is linked in scripture with the Holy Spirit as the unseen source of energy and power. The priests had the daily task of replenishing the oil and trimming the wicks that burnt in the bowls holding the oil. We do not have any dimensions for the lampstand. All we know is what it was made of, how it was ornamented, and where it stood. It shares this feature with the laver. In addition the Lampstand, like the laver and the Mercy Seat, was made of solid metal.

The Altar of Incense

Also known as the Golden Altar, it was made of shittim wood overlaid with gold. It stood before the veil. It was a far smaller altar than the Brazen Altar that stood in the Court.[26] It was not used to offer animals but to burn incense.

Coals from the Brazen Altar were taken into the Holy Place in a censer, a small vessel that contained the live coals, and placed on the top of the altar. The priest would pour a bowl of incense on the live coals atop the altar. Thereupon a cloud of incense would rise up. Unlike the smoke of the altar which would rise to heaven, the incense would fill the Holy Place.

Incense represents the prayers of the people. The connection between prayer and incense is made clear in Psalm 141:2, Rev. 5:8 and 8:3. This indicates that prayers are not demanding and tiresome to God but pleasing to Him. Since anything emanating from the heart of man is to an extent tainted, the altar was purified yearly by an act of atonement (Ex. 30:10).

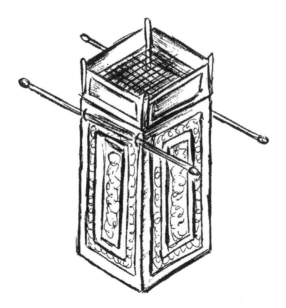

---

[26] The Golden Altar was square and about 3 feet high.

The Order of the Vessels

The book of Exodus begins in ch 25 with the most important vessel, the Ark, followed by the Table and the Candlestick. There is no mention of the Golden Altar until ch 30. Why are all three not mentioned together? This may be because it served a different purpose. The other two vessels represented the Lord and His ability to illuminate and provide for His people. The Golden Altar by contrast depicts man reaching out to God through prayer. Although it is not described in Exodus 25 it stood beside the Ark, separated only by the Veil. If its importance is determined by its proximity to the Ark, it ranks before the other two vessels in the Holy Place.

The Table of Shewbread

23 Thou shalt also make a table of shittim wood: two cubits shall be the length thereof, and a cubit the breadth thereof, and a cubit and a half the height thereof. 24 And thou shalt overlay it with pure gold, and make thereto a crown of gold round about. 25 And thou shalt make unto it a border of an hand breadth round about, and thou shalt make a golden crown to the border thereof round about. 26 And thou shalt make for it four rings of gold, and put the rings in the four corners that are on the four feet thereof. 27 Over against the border shall the rings be for places of the staves to bear the table. 28 And thou shalt make the staves of shittim wood, and overlay them with gold, that the table may be borne with them. 29 And thou shalt make the dishes thereof, and spoons thereof, and covers thereof, and bowls thereof, to cover withal: of pure gold shalt thou make them. 30 And thou shalt set upon the table shewbread before me alway.

Ex. 25:23-30

5 And thou shalt take fine flour, and bake twelve cakes thereof: two tenth deals shall be in one cake. 6 And thou shalt set them in two rows, six on a row, upon the pure table before the LORD. 7 And thou shalt put pure frankincense upon each row, that it may be on the bread for a memorial, even an offering made by fire unto the LORD. 8 Every sabbath he shall set it in order before the LORD continually, being taken from the children of Israel by an everlasting covenant.

Lev. 24:5-8

The Golden Lampstand

31 And thou shalt make a candlestick of pure gold: of beaten work shall the candlestick be made: his shaft, and his branches, his bowls, his knops, and his flowers, shall be of the same. 32 And six branches shall come out of the sides of it; three branches of the candlestick out of the one side, and three branches of the candlestick out of the other side: 33 Three bowls made like unto almonds, with a knop and

a flower in one branch; and three bowls made like almonds in the other branch, *with* a knop and a flower: so in the six branches that come out of the candlestick. ³⁴ And in the candlestick *shall be* four bowls made like unto almonds, *with* their knops and their flowers. ³⁵ And *there shall be* a knop under two branches of the same, and a knop under two branches of the same, and a knop under two branches of the same, according to the six branches that proceed out of the candlestick. ³⁶ Their knops and their branches shall be of the same: all it *shall be* one beaten work *of* pure gold. ³⁷ And thou shalt make the seven lamps thereof: and they shall light the lamps thereof, that they may give light over against it. ³⁸ And the tongs thereof, and the snuffdishes thereof, *shall be* of pure gold. ³⁹ *Of* a talent of pure gold shall he make it, with all these vessels. ⁴⁰ And look that thou make *them* after their pattern, which was shewed thee in the mount.

Ex. 25:31-48

The Altar of Incense

¹ And thou shalt make an altar to burn incense upon: *of* shittim wood shalt thou make it. ² A cubit *shall be* the length thereof, and a cubit the breadth thereof; foursquare shall it be: and two cubits *shall be* the height thereof: the horns thereof *shall be* of the same. ³ And thou shalt overlay it with pure gold, the top thereof, and the sides thereof round about, and the horns thereof; and thou shalt make unto it a crown of gold round about. ⁴ And two golden rings shalt thou make to it under the crown of it, by the two corners thereof, upon the two sides of it shalt thou make *it*; and they shall be for places for the staves to bear it withal. ⁵ And thou shalt make the staves *of* shittim wood, and overlay them with gold. ⁶ And thou shalt put it before the vail that *is* by the ark of the testimony, before the mercy seat that *is* over the testimony, where I will meet with thee. ⁷And Aaron shall burn thereon sweet incense every morning: when he dresseth the lamps, he shall burn incense upon it. ⁸ And when

KEY SCRIPTURES

Aaron lighteth the lamps at even, he shall burn incense upon it, a perpetual incense before the LORD throughout your generations. [9] Ye shall offer no strange incense thereon, nor burnt sacrifice, nor meat offering; neither shall ye pour drink offering thereon. [10] And Aaron shall make an atonement upon the horns of it once in a year with the blood of the sin offering of atonements: once in the year shall he make atonement upon it throughout your generations: it *is* most holy unto the LORD.

Ex. 30:1-10

[35] And you shall set the table outside the veil, and the lampstand on the south side of the tabernacle opposite the table, and you shall put the table on the north side.

Ex. 26:35 (E.S.V.)

[1] Then verily the first *covenant* had also ordinances of divine service, and a worldly sanctuary. [2] For there was a tabernacle made; the first, wherein *was* the candlestick, and the table, and the shewbread; which is called the sanctuary. [3] And after the second veil, the tabernacle which is called the Holiest of all; [4] Which had the golden censer, and the ark of the covenant overlaid round about with gold, wherein *was* the golden pot that had manna, and Aaron's rod that budded, and the tables of the covenant; [5] And over it the cherubims of glory shadowing the mercyseat; of which we cannot now speak particularly.

Heb. 9:1-5

[3] And another angel came and stood at the altar, having a golden censer; and there was given unto him much incense, that he should offer *it* with the prayers of all saints upon the golden altar which was before the throne. [4] And the smoke of the incense, *which came* with the prayers of the saints, ascended up before God out of the angel's hand.

Rev. 8:3-4

KEY QUOTES

...the lampstand is to be made of beaten gold...from this we learn that in order for the lampstand to shed forth its light...the gold must be beaten...The bringing of the Light of the World to mankind was a costly thing for the Godhead...The One who supplies the power to the Light...is hidden all the time...we cannot see the oil in the lampstand but we can see the light.

Only two items of furniture in the tabernacle had no provision made for their transportation. Every item except the laver and the lampstand was equipped with rings through which staves were inserted so that the sons of Kohath could carry them...were the lampstand and the laver to be left behind?...surely the lesson must be this. You and I cannot carry round the Holy Spirit where we wish. He must take the lead and we must follow.

CH Raven[27]

The horns of the altar of incense were not just for decoration but served a specific purpose in relations to the blood of sacrifice. First on the Day of atonement...the high priest took some of the blood... and put it on the horns of the altar to "make an atonement" (Ex 30:10; Lev. 16:18). Second the altar served as a place of expiation for the sins of the priests and the congregation (Lev. 4:7, 18-19)...The Golden Altar thus represented the place of intercession before the Lord...the blood when applied to the altar gave the incense of prayer its value.

David Levy[28]

The measurements of the Table are carefully given... the height is the same as the Ark (Ex 25:10). In length and breadth the Ark exceeded the Table by half a cubit. Our communion at the Table never comes up to what the Mercy Seat and Ark are to God. What He rests on and finds there far exceeds our realisations.

Walter Scott[29]

[27] God's Sanctuary. Meditations on the Tabernacle. (John Ritchie) p. 180.
[28] The Tabernacle. Shadows of the Messiah (Friends of Israel Gospel Ministry) p. 66.
[29] The Tabernacle. Its structure and symbolism (Ambassador) p. 105.

KEY QUESTIONS

1. What did the loaves on the Table represent?

2. What does the oil in the Lamp symbolise?

3. What does the incense symbolise?

4. Why were these vessels made of gold whereas the vessels in the court were made of brass?

The Ark of The Covenant and Mercy Seat

Key Points

- The Ark of the Covenant together with its cover, the mercy seat, was the only vessel in the Holy of Holies.

- It contained the Ten Commandments, manna from the wilderness and Aaron's rod.

- Blood was sprinkled annually on the mercy seat on the Day of Atonement.

- The mercy seat speaks of Christ's death for sin.

In the Holy of Holies was the most sacred vessel in the Tabernacle. It was the Ark of the Covenant.[30] Its special status is marked out by its location and the fact that the High Priest was only permitted to appear before it once a year. While other vessels such as the Altar of Burnt Offering and the Laver were replaced when the Temple was built, the Ark was retained.

The "Ark" was an oblong box made of shittim wood. While the Table and Altar of Incense were overlaid on their exterior with gold, the Ark was overlaid on both the exterior and interior with gold. The lid by contrast was made of solid gold. It was more than a mere lid. It had a specific

---

[30] In Exodus it is usually called the "ark" or "the ark of the testimony". Elsewhere in scripture it is called "the ark of the covenant", the "ark of wood" and "the ark of the Lord".

function as the place where sin was put away or atoned. Translators have sought to express the idea of sin being put away from before God by a variety of terms. The A.V. entitles it the "mercy seat". Other translations use different language such as "the atonement cover" [N.I.V.], the "atonement lid" [NET Bible]. The lid of the ark was the place where the blood was sprinkled on the Day of Atonement (Lev. 16). On it were fixed two angelic figures, the cherubim. Depictions of them vary. Sometimes they are depicted as kneeling and sometimes standing. In some illustrations their whole body is visible and in others their torso, faces and wings. We do not know exactly what Moses saw in his vision or how the craftsmen depicted the cherubim. What we do know is that they had wings which stretched towards the centre of the ark and that the faces of the cherubim looked inwards. This posture indicates that angelic attention is focussed on the spot where the blood is shed. The Scriptures indicate that the Lord dwelt between these cherubim.[31] He is described as the One who sat between the cherubim. On this account the word *kapporet* is translated as "mercy seat" indicating that the One enthroned between the cherubim could have mercy on account of the shedding of blood.

Inside the Ark were, in addition to the unbroken Tables of the Law, a pot of manna and Aaron's rod that budded. Ex. 16:33 says the pot was laid up "before the Lord" which some have taken to contradict Heb. 9:4. However if this instruction was given before the Ark was built it may have been placed before the Lord until the Ark was completed and then placed inside the Ark. Aaron's rod was similarly placed "before the testimony" (Num. 17:4) which Hebrews 9 indicates was in the Ark. It signified God's approval of the Levites as priests after the complaints expressed in Numbers 16. Each tribe placed a rod before the Lord and God miraculously caused Aaron's rod to bud.

The Ark is the vessel that most clearly depicts the Lord Jesus. The shittim wood grew out of the soil of earth and speaks of his humanity (Ex 37:1; Heb. 2:14). It was overlaid with gold (Ex 37:2) which speaks of His deity (Jn 1:1, 14). The Mercy Seat is a picture of His death (Rom. 3:25) and the tables of the Law inside the Ark remind us that the law was "within" His heart (Psalm 40:8). It was in the midst (Num. 2:17) as He was (Rev. 1:13; Matt 18:20). The Ark had a triumphal entry (1 Chron. 15) as did the Lord Jesus (Matt. 21:1). It crossed Kidron (2 Sam 15:24) and

---

[31] 1 Sam. 4:4; 2 Sam. 6:2; 2 Kings 19:15; Psalm 80:1; 99:1.

so did He (Jn. 18:1). It was taken by the enemy (1 Sam 4:11; Psalm 78:60, 61) as He was (Mk 14:46) and was abandoned by Israel (1 Sam 4:10) in the same way His disciples forsook Him (Mk 14:50). Dagon fell before the Ark (1 Sam 5:3, 4) as the Lord Jesus' enemies fell before Him (Jn 18:6). The ark was brought in to its place at last (2 Chron. 5:7; 35:3) as was the Lord Jesus when received back to heaven (Heb. 1:3; Rev. 21:3).

KEY SCRIPTURES

¹⁰ And they shall make an ark *of* shittim wood: two cubits and a half *shall be* the length thereof, and a cubit and a half the breadth thereof, and a cubit and a half the height thereof. ¹¹ And thou shalt overlay it with pure gold, within and without shalt thou overlay it, and shalt make upon it a crown of gold round about. ¹² And thou shalt cast four rings of gold for it, and put *them* in the four corners thereof; and two rings *shall be* in the one side of it, and two rings in the other side of it. ¹³ And thou shalt make staves *of* shittim wood, and overlay them with gold. ¹⁴ And thou shalt put the staves into the rings by the sides of the ark, that the ark may be borne with them. ¹⁵ The staves shall be in the rings of the ark: they shall not be taken from it. ¹⁶ And thou shalt put into the ark the testimony which I shall give thee. ¹⁷ And thou shalt make a mercy seat *of* pure gold: two cubits and a half *shall be* the length thereof, and a cubit and a half the breadth thereof. ¹⁸ And thou shalt make two cherubims *of* gold, *of* beaten work shalt thou make them, in the two ends of the mercy seat. ¹⁹ And make one cherub on the one end, and the other cherub on the other end: *even* of the mercy seat shall ye make the cherubims on the two ends thereof. ²⁰ And the cherubims shall stretch forth *their* wings on high, covering the mercy seat with their wings, and their faces *shall look* one to another; toward the mercy seat shall the faces of the cherubims be. ²¹ And thou shalt put the mercy seat above upon the ark; and in the ark thou shalt put the testimony that I shall give thee. ²² And there I will meet with thee, and I will commune with thee from above the mercy seat, from between the two cherubims which *are* upon the ark of the testimony, of all *things* which I will give thee in commandment unto the children of Israel.

Ex. 25:10-22

² And the LORD said unto Moses, Speak unto Aaron thy brother, that he come not at all times into the holy *place* within the vail before

the mercy seat, which *is* upon the ark; that he die not: for I will appear in the cloud upon the mercy seat.

Lev. 16:2

² For there was a tabernacle made; the first, wherein *was* the candlestick, and the table, and the shewbread; which is called the sanctuary. ³ And after the second veil, the tabernacle which is called the Holiest of all; ⁴ Which had the golden censer, and the ark of the covenant overlaid round about with gold, wherein *was* the golden pot that had manna, and Aaron's rod that budded, and the tables of the covenant; ⁵ And over it the cherubims of glory shadowing the mercyseat; of which we cannot now speak particularly. ⁶ Now when these things were thus ordained, the priests went always into the first tabernacle, accomplishing the service *of God*. ⁷ But into the second *went* the high priest alone once every year, not without blood, which he offered for himself, and *for* the errors of the people:

Heb. 9:2-7

¹⁶ And it shall come to pass, when ye be multiplied and increased in the land, in those days, saith the LORD, they shall say no more, The ark of the covenant of the LORD: neither shall it come to mind: neither shall they remember it; neither shall they visit *it*; neither shall *that* be done any more.

Jer. 3:16

¹⁹ And the temple of God was opened in heaven, and there was seen in his temple the ark of his testament: and there were lightnings, and voices, and thunderings, and an earthquake, and great hail.

Rev. 11:19

KEY QUOTES

The mercy seat was made of pure gold... no wood was used in its manufacture. This means that what is in view is not so much the divinity of our Lord as related to His humanity but rather His divinity in relation to righteousness. Without divine righteousness being satisfied by the shedding and application of blood, there would be no outflowing of grace to guilty men... What does the Mercy Seat mean and what does it stand for? We learn from both O.T. and N.T. that it was the place of propitiation. Upon the mercy seat was the blood of propitiation sprinkled every year on the Day of atonement... (Rom. 3:25; 1 Jn. 4:10)... because of the blood sprinkled mercy seat we can know reconciliation, forgiveness, justification and peace.[32]

Stephen Olford

Shittim wood... in many scriptures Christ is referred to under the simile of a tree or parts thereof - "a tender plant (sapling)" and a "root out of dry ground" (Isaiah 53:2)."there shall come forth a shoot out of the stock of Jesse and a branch out of his roots shall be fruitful" (Isa 11:1)... the shittim tree was the only timber bearing tree that could grow in the desert. It had a powerful taproot that grew downward in search of water and when it found its subterranean source of sustenance, it spread out its roots by the water and was not dependent upon moisture above ground. It had a secret source of supply.... The Lord Jesus did not depend upon His circumstances or surroundings for support. His delight was in the law of the Lord... the world around Him was and still is a moral desert... He grew and become a strong and fruitful for God... Another natural feature about shittim wood is that it is indestructible. I am told it can lie in water for centuries and it will not even have a wormhole in it. It is truly "incorruptible wood". Therefor it symbolizes the qualities of the humanity of Christ. His perfect, spotless, deathless, sinless humanity.[33]

Laurence Chambers

[32] The Tabernacle. Camping with God (Loizeaux Bros) p. 138.
[33] Tabernacle Studies (John Ritchie) pp. 38-39.

KEY QUESTIONS

1. Why did God require the Israelites to use shittim (acacia) wood for the Ark?

2. Why was the mercy seat made of gold?

3. On what day did the High Priest sprinkle blood on the mercy seat?

4. What was the "covenant" placed inside the ark?

The Veil, the Boards, the Curtains

Key Points
- The coverings on the Tabernacle served to protect the vessels from the weather and to screen them from public view.

- The curtains and boards were designed to be dismantled and stowed away easily and quickly.

- The colours of the fabrics spoke of heaven (blue), royalty (purple), sacrifice (scarlet) and purity (white).

- The silver used in the Tabernacle represented the idea that God had purchased or redeemed His people.

The Curtains – Protecting Holiness

The sheets that draped over the tabernacle are called "curtains". The first curtain was made of white linen interwoven with blue, purple and scarlet thread. Embroidered cherubim were stitched into the material. Above it was another covering of goats' hair, followed by another covering of rams' skins dyed red and finally the curtain of skins from a creature that may have been a porpoise or dugong.

The three outer coverings were designed to protect the Tabernacle from rain and other forms of inclement weather. The outer skin was waterproof and the other two layers provided further protection. The inner curtain however was designed to beautify. While it may be that only God was intended to "see" its beauties, it is preferable to see them as designed to be seen by the priests as they ministered within the Tabernacle. If the boards were in a lattice arrangement this would have been possible.

Although the curtains may have looked like four large sheets of fabric, in fact they were all composed of smaller parts joined together. The first curtain was composed of 10 mini-sheets (28 x 4 cubits). They were sown together into two large sheets each composed of 5 parts. The two large sections were then joined by clasps. These golden clasps ("taches") hooked through loops of blue that were attached to the end of the curtain pieces. The fact that the sheets could be taken apart made them easier to transport. When the curtains were transported they could be unhooked and folded away. The curtain of goats' hair was longer than the first curtain and was designed to drape down to the wilderness floor at the rear and sides of the Tabernacle. It was folded back at the entrance. There is not much detail about how the final two coverings were made. Presumably they were made of individual skins or hides stitched together.

The exterior curtains were designed to protect the holy vessels and the beautiful inner curtain. God ever protects what is of value to Him.

The Boards – Promoting Holiness
The boards were the "hard shell" of the Tabernacle. These wooden uprights gave it its shape and structure. The boards ran along three sides of the Tabernacle – to the north and south and to the west. The east side was not boarded. A "door" (or screen) permitted entrance to the Holy Place and a further veil hung across the entrance to the Holy of Holies.[34] The roof was made of the coverings of the Tabernacle. There was no flooring. The desert floor was the surface on which the priests walked. Whether the boards were solid is not specified. Many think that they were a lattice-like structure of the sort depicted in the illustrations. The principal reason for thinking this is that the embroidery on the curtains and the cherubim would then be visible to the priests within the tabernacle. If not they would be completely obscured by the boards on the inside and by the coverings from the outside. A lattice structure would also make the structure lighter and more portable.

---

[34] The "gate" of the Tabernacle gave entrance to the courtyard, the "door" gave entrance to the Tabernacle itself and the "veil" gave entrance to the Holy of Holies.

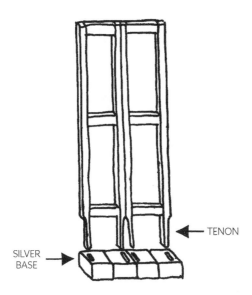

The boards had small tenons or rods that protruded from their base and these were inserted into silver bases with sockets. These enabled the boards to stand upright.

The illustration below shows solid boards braced by 5 long poles that ran along the length of the boards and held in place by golden rings.

The Veil – Preserving Holiness
The veil (A.V. – "vail") hung between the Holy Place and the Holy of Holies. While usually the fine twined linen is mentioned first followed by blue, purple and scarlet, in the veil the blue, purple and scarlet come first. So they may have been the dominant threads. Into it were woven representations of the cherubim. This is not the case at the door of the Tabernacle. But as the cherubim guarded the Garden of Eden after the Fall (Gen. 3:24), so these angelic creatures guarded God's presence in the Tabernacle. The High Priest entered once a year on the Day of Atonement (Lev. 16:2, 12 and 15). There are indications that Moses when he communicated with God directly may have had special access (Num. 7:89).

The Tabernacle – Portraying Christ
The unattractive exterior of the Tabernacle reminds us that the Lord Jesus when He "tabernacled" among us did not come in glory or power. There was no

"beauty that we should desire him" (Is. 53:2). The beauty was internal. Inside the Tabernacle the white linen and coloured threads that speak of His attributes were visible to the priest.

The Tabernacle can also be viewed as a picture of the assembly. We can see that each board was secured in the sockets of silver. Silver in scripture is often linked with purchase or the redemption of people or objects. Silver was a common form of currency and was used (a) to "purchase" Joseph (Gen. 37:28) and (b) the Lord (Matt. 26:15). Silver was the metal used when Israel bought its "freedom" and redeemed itself (Ex. 30:11-16; 38:25). The vast amount of silver they contributed was the principal source of the silver used in the Tabernacle. So when we see the tenons inserted into the sockets rather than into the soil of the wilderness, we see that our place in the assembly is based on what God has done for us in the redemptive work of Christ.

The boards were all of course perfectly in line and stood in bases made of silver. We should be the same. The assembly's members should stand "shoulder to shoulder" and work in perfect harmony.

The veil was what stood between the priests and the presence of God. It preserved God's holiness by keeping man at a distance. Equally it was the veil through which the High Priest passed in order to gain admittance on the Day of Atonement. In Hebrews the veil is likened to the humanity of the Lord Jesus. It was because of His humanity and His sacrifice on the cross that we have been able to enter God's presence. After the Lord died, the veil in Herod's temple was torn from the top to the bottom. God did the rending since the tear began at the top and went to the bottom. This tear does not signify any physical rending of the Lord's flesh. It signifies instead the opening of the way into God's presence.

 **KEY SCRIPTURES**

1 Moreover thou shalt make the tabernacle *with* ten curtains *of* fine twined linen, and blue, and purple, and scarlet: *with* cherubims of cunning work shalt thou make them. 2 The length of one curtain *shall be* eight and twenty cubits, and the breadth of one curtain four cubits: and every one of the curtains shall have one measure.

Ex. 26:1-2

15 And thou shalt make boards for the tabernacle *of* shittim wood standing up. 16 Ten cubits *shall be* the length of a board, and a cubit and a half *shall be* the breadth of one board. 17 Two tenons *shall there be* in one board, set in order one against another: thus shalt thou make for all the boards of the tabernacle.

Ex. 26:15-17

31 And thou shalt make a vail *of* blue, and purple, and scarlet, and fine twined linen of cunning work: with cherubims shall it be made: 32 And thou shalt hang it upon four pillars of shittim *wood* overlaid with gold: their hooks *shall be of* gold, upon the four sockets of silver. 33 And thou shalt hang up the vail under the taches, that thou mayest bring in thither within the vail the ark of the testimony: and the vail shall divide unto you between the holy *place* and the most holy.

Ex. 26:31-33

36 And thou shalt make an hanging for the door of the tent, *of* blue, and purple, and scarlet, and fine twined linen, wrought with needlework. 37 And thou shalt make for the hanging five pillars *of* shittim *wood*, and overlay them with gold, *and* their hooks *shall be of* gold: and thou shalt cast five sockets of brass for them.

Ex. 26:36-37

KEY SCRIPTURES

[50] Jesus, when he had cried again with a loud voice, yielded up the ghost. [51] And, behold, the veil of the temple was rent in twain from the top to the bottom; and the earth did quake, and the rocks rent;

Mt. 27:50-51

[18] the hope set before us: [19] Which *hope* we have as an anchor of the soul, both sure and stedfast, and which entereth into that within the veil;

Heb. 6:18-19

[19] Having therefore, brethren, boldness to enter into the holiest by the blood of Jesus, [20] By a new and living way, which he hath consecrated for us, through the veil, that is to say, his flesh; [21] And *having* an high priest over the house of God; [22] Let us draw near with a true heart in full assurance of faith.

Heb. 10:19-22

[16] let us walk by the same rule, let us mind the same thing.

Phil. 3:16

KEY QUOTES

Each board of shittim wood overlaid with gold seems to portray the Lord Jesus Himself, the Son of God, the Son of Man. The shittim wood, incorruptible wood being a shadow of that great truth, that he "partook of flesh and blood".... And at the same time "the Son of the Highest"... the gold also portrays that He is "the Mighty God"... each board of the tabernacle, each bar, each pillar reiterates again and again these great verities... the boards are like ribs of the truth, the massive frame work, without which no dwelling place of God could be created, no meeting place between God and man could be provided.[35]

Henry Soltau

What a privilege belongs to us this day! God who formerly shut Himself in and man out, now says "I want you to enter" and "I want you to draw near". Indeed He says "enter with boldness" and draw near "with full assurance". In Hebrews 10 the veil is neither rent nor removed for this is not God coming out but we entering and drawing near. God has come out without reserve as seen in the rent veil but we cannot enter through the rent veil but through the veil which is still there as far as our entry is concerned.[36]

Albert Leckie

---

[35] The Tabernacle, the Priesthood and the Offerings (Kregel Publications) p. 76.
[36] The Tabernacle and the Offerings (Precious Seed Publications) p. 111.

KEY QUESTIONS

1. Why were figures of angels stitched into the fabric of the inner curtain?

2. What did the boards of the Tabernacle rest on?

3. How many entrances were there in the Tabernacle?

4. What purpose did the "taches" or clasps serve?

The Courtyard

Key Points

- The Courtyard was a large open air space where worshippers offered their sacrifices.

- It was enclosed by white hangings that provided privacy and whose colour emphasised the holiness of the Tabernacle.

- The gate was embroidered with blue, purple and scarlet and was about 30 feet wide, stressing God's

The Courtyard's Curtilage

The outer perimeter of the Tabernacle consisted of sheets of linen stretched between poles of wood. These linen walls were about 8 feet high (5 cubits)[37] and the poles were footed in sockets of brass (bronze). The length of courtyard was 100 cubits (about 159 feet). That is roughly half the length of a football pitch. It was 50 cubits wide.

The linen sheets or hangings had hooks that were attached to silver bands (fillets) that encircled each pole. In order to keep the poles upright they were footed with sockets of brass. They were also braced

[37] Ex. 27:18.

willingness to admit people to the Tabernacle.

- The Courtyard was the space where the Brazen Altar and Laver were situated and where most of the activity of the Tabernacle took place.

with cords which were fixed to pegs (pins) which were driven into the wilderness. These cords acted like the guy ropes that are used to keep tents upright.

The sheets provided privacy for the worshippers and the priests. They were so high that no one could see in. Equally no one inside could see out. There were no distractions inside the Tabernacle. The courtyard was a large open area. The Tent lay towards the rear of the Courtyard. There was plenty of room for the work of sacrifice. The use of brass sockets for the poles was in line with the fact that the courtyard was the area where God's judgement against sin was emphasised. The main metal was brass with only the fillets being made of silver. In the Holy Place and Holy of Holies gold and silver were used. The vessels were of gold and the fittings were made of silver.

The Courtyard's Curtain

The only break in the Courtyard was at the "gate" of the Tabernacle. It was 20 cubits (about 30 feet) wide. This meant that it could admit large numbers of people and their sacrifices. The gate was made of coloured fabric. The sheets must have been either pulled to one side or draped so that they could be pulled aside so that the worshipper could gain admittance. Four wooden pillars stood at the gate. The door of the Tabernacle was narrower. It was 10 cubits wide and there were 5 pillars meaning that there was 2.5 cubits between each pole. There was therefore sufficient width to remove the Ark if it was necessary to carry it out while the Tabernacle remained standing.

The Courtyard's Colours

White was the Tabernacle's predominant colour. A worshipper would be struck by the long lengths of white linen surrounding the Tabernacle. The Tabernacle itself was quite drab in appearance and the white linen must have been quite a contrast. This was designed to emphasise the holiness of the place.

Like the veil and the door of the Tabernacle, the hangings at the gate were woven with blue, purple and scarlet.   These colours signified heaven (blue), royalty (purple) and sacrifice (scarlet). The Tabernacle was the place where heaven was brought close to man. It was the place where God's authority was recognised. Israel had no king in the wilderness. They were led by God and His representative Moses, a Levite. It was also the place where sacrificial blood flowed, represented by the scarlet.

The Courtyard's Covering

The Courtyard's floor was the Wilderness floor and its canopy was the sky. The terrain through which Israel passed in the forty years in the wilderness was often inhospitable so stones, dust and sand would have covered its floor at most of their stops.[38]   The fact that the desert floor was beneath his feet reminded the worshipper that he belonged to a fallen world. The sky above his head reminded him he was part of creation.

---

[38] Numbers 33 lists the stopping places between Egypt and Canaan.

KEY SCRIPTURES

⁹ And thou shalt make the court of the tabernacle: for the south side southward *there shall be* hangings for the court *of* fine twined linen of an hundred cubits long for one side: ¹⁰ And the twenty pillars thereof and their twenty sockets *shall be of* brass; the hooks of the pillars and their fillets *shall be of* silver. ¹¹ And likewise for the north side in length *there shall be* hangings of an hundred *cubits* long, and his twenty pillars and their twenty sockets *of* brass; the hooks of the pillars and their fillets *of* silver. ¹² And *for* the breadth of the court on the west side *shall be* hangings of fifty cubits: their pillars ten, and their sockets ten. ¹³ And the breadth of the court on the east side eastward *shall be* fifty cubits.

Ex. 27:9-13

⁵ holiness becometh thine house, O LORD, for ever.

Ps. 93:5

¹⁴ The hangings of one side *of the gate shall be* fifteen cubits: their pillars three, and their sockets three. ¹⁵ And on the other side *shall be* hangings fifteen *cubits*: their pillars three, and their sockets three. ¹⁶ And for the gate of the court *shall be* an hanging of twenty cubits, of blue, and purple, and scarlet, and fine twined linen, wrought with needlework: *and* their pillars *shall be* four, and their sockets four. ¹⁷ All the pillars round about the court *shall be* filleted with silver; their hooks *shall be of* silver, and their sockets *of* brass. ¹⁸ The length of the court *shall be* an hundred cubits, and the breadth fifty every where, and the height five cubits *of* fine twined linen, and their sockets *of* brass.

Ex. 27:14-18

⁹ I am the door: by me if any man enter in, he shall be saved,

Jn. 10:9

 **KEY QUOTES**

The order in which the commands concerning the Tabernacle and its vessels were given by Jehovah to Moses... was from within to without.... The order in which our souls apprehend the truth is from without to within. We begin with the Court and its gates and travel inward past the brazen altar and the laver and onwards till we reach the throne of God.[39]

John Ritchie

The Israelite who came to the brazen altar with his sacrifice or gifts must first pass through the gate of the court. The priest that placed incense on the golden altar within the tabernacle entered through the second door curtain. The high priest who alone had access into the holiest, passed through the veil, the third hanging of the same kind; and realised the thrice repeated truth of the only way to God.[40]

Henry Soltau

[39] The Tabernacle in the Wilderness (John Ritchie) p 18.
[40] The Tabernacle, the Priesthood and the Offerings (Kregel) p. 118.

KEY QUESTIONS

1. Which vessels were situated in the courtyard?

2. What was the colour of the perimeter curtain?

3. How wide was the Tabernacle gate?

4. What was the approximate size of the whole Tabernacle?

The Priesthood

Key Points

- The priest was an intermediary between man and God and offered sacrifices in the Tabernacle.

- The priesthood was drawn from the tribe of Levi and the family of Aaron.

The Purpose of a Priest

Although as we have seen the Tabernacle was God's dwelling place among His people, the veil, screen, gate and curtains showed that a respectful distance was maintained between man and the immediate presence of God. Although the ordinary man could not enter God's presence, He established a group of men who were permitted to enter on their behalf. These were the priests. The priest was an intermediary

- The other Levites looked after the fabric and transportation of the Tabernacle.

- In the N.T. the believer does not need an earthly priest because access to God is secured by the priestly work of Christ.

between man and God and acted on his behalf in offering sacrifices. The priesthood was also there to ensure that God's ways were followed carefully. The laws that circumscribed approach to God required a trained body of men who could be relied on to know and obey the Law.[41]   Thus in the O.T. the ordinary Israelite could not worship with the freedom we do. No priest was needed for basic spiritual exercises such as prayer. But sacrifice necessitated a priest. Although "high places" were established in a variety of places after Israel entered the Land, it would appear that God intended there to be one altar and one place of worship first at the Tabernacle and then at the Temple in Jerusalem.[42]   Priests were necessary for the Nation's system of worship.

The Place of the Priest

While there were evidently people who functioned as priests before the Law,[4] it was only with the giving of the Law that a priestly class was established. The priests were drawn from the male members of one family. This was the family of Aaron. Although Moses his brother had many privileges[44] he was not a member of the priesthood.

Every priest was a Levite but not every Levite was a priest. In fact at the inauguration of the Priesthood very few were priests. At that time the males in the tribe of Levi numbered about 22 000[45] of which only Aaron, Nadab, Abihu, Eleazar and Ithamar were priests. Shortly afterwards Nadab and Abihu were slain so for most of the time Israel was in the Wilderness there were only three priests

---

[41] That did no prevent the priests getting it wrong – see Lev. 10:16.
[42] Deut. 12:11-14.
[43] Ex. 18:1,12 – Jethro, Moses father in law, is described as a "priest" (Ex. 2:16). From Ex. 19:22 it seems there were people acting as priests before the Priesthood was set up.
[44] He anointed the priests and it seems was at times able to enter the Holy of Holies; cf. Ps. 99:6.
[45] Num. 3:39 – 22 000.

The purpose of the role was to serve in the Tabernacle. They sacrificed animals, tended the Altar, trimmed the lamps and maintained the Table.

Levites were responsible for the fabric[46] of the Tabernacle including its erection, dismantling and transport.[47] It seems that they shared with priests the duty of instructing Israel[48] and were maintained by the tithe, a form of taxation.[49]   Thus while the other tribes became farmers and fishermen after settling in Canaan, Levites and priests became Israel's educators.[50] This was a major responsibility and may explain why the numbers of Levites exceeded the number of priests. They had no tribal territory[51] and lived in towns scattered through Israel.

In the N.T. priests regularly encountered the Lord. On the whole they were not favorably disposed to Him though there were exceptions.[52] In the post-resurrection period many priests believed that the Lord Jesus was after all their promised Messiah.[53]

The Prominent Priest
The senior figure in the priestly community was the High Priest. The first to occupy the role was Aaron. The High Priesthood was an office handed from father to son, with the eldest son being the heir. Since Nadab and Abihu died prematurely, Eleazar, Aaron's third son, succeeded to the High Priesthood when Aaron died.[54]   After they entered Canaan the spiritual state of the Nation deteriorated and during the period of the Judges there is little to suggest that the priesthood provided effective spiritual leadership.[55]   As the epoch of the judges came to an end it is clear the Tabernacle was still functioning at Shiloh. 1st Samuel introduces us to Eli. Though he is not called a High Priest that is probably what he was. His young assistant Samuel wore an ephod and engaged in priestly work even though under-age[56] and from the tribe of Ephraim.[57] In the

---

[46] Num. 3:25-37.
[47] Num. 1:50, 51.
[48] Deut. 33:10; Mal. 2:7.
[49] Num. 18:24; Lev. 27:30.
[50] 2 Ch. 35:3.
[51] Num. 18:20.
[52] Lk. 1:5-6.
[53] Acts 6:7.
[54] Num. 20:23-29.
[55] Jud. 17-19.
[56] Num. 8:24-26.
[57] 1 Sam. 1:1. Some think Samuel was a Levite (see 1 Chron 6:23-30) and that 1 Sam. 1:1 merely means that his family lived in Ephraim.

reign of David Abiathar and Zadok were prominent. Although the expression "high priest" is not used, the clear implication of 1 Kings 2:27 is that Abiathar had been functioning in that capacity and was replaced at Solomon's behest by Zadok.[58] The line of Zadok is the line that is prophesied to have the privilege of priesthood in the Millennial Temple.[59]   By the time of the Lord the office of High Priest seems to have moved out of the Aaronic line and become a political appointment.

The garments of the High Priest have attracted a lot of attention. As the Tabernacle was designed to teach Israel so too the garments of the High Priest were a source of instruction. The names of the tribes were engraved on 12 stones that were over the High Priest's heart. This no doubt was intended to show the people that they were the object of priestly care and divine love. The names were also etched into two stones worn on the High Priest's shoulders showing that the priest and Jehovah upheld them. The only writing, apart from the etched names of the tribes, in the whole Tabernacle system was found on a circlet of gold round the High Priest's head. It said "Holiness unto the Lord". This stressed the principle that governed the High Priest's life and the chief object of the Tabernacle. Sound was on the whole lacking in the Tabernacle – no songs were sung until the Temple was built. No confessions were required – except the annual confession on the Day of Atonement.[60] The only sound required in the Tabernacle was the sound of golden bells. Since they were sewn to the hem of the High Priest's garment their sound was a proof to those who could not see him beyond the screen to the Holy Place that he was still alive and ministering for the people.[61]   On the Day of Atonement he changed into another outfit. It was white from top to toe. This was to emphasise that on that day the main issue was the atonement of the Nation's sins and their consequent forgiveness. There are many other lessons to be gleaned from his garments which are beyond the scope of this short introduction.[62]

---

[58] According to 1 Chron. 24:3 Abiathar was descended from Ithamar, Aaron's 4th son and Zadok was descended from Eleazar Aaron's 3rd son and his successor; cf. Mk. 2:26.
[59] Ezek. 44:15, 16.
[60] Lev. 16:21; the confession of Lev. 5:5 is not in the Tabernacle.
[61] Ex. 28:35. Some think that the bell announced the arrival of the High Priest and note that the bells rang while he was in the Holy Place (not the Holy of Holies where he did not wear the garments for glory and beauty).
[62] For a more detailed treatment see e.g. "These are the Garments" CW Slemming.

The Present Priesthood

In the N.T. the need for an earthly priesthood is abolished. The Lord Jesus ended their work of sacrifice by His death on the cross. Their priesthood was displaced by His priesthood. He was not of Levitical stock but came from the tribe of Judah. His priesthood Hebrews tells us was of a different order and is paralleled to the priesthood of Melchizedek, a priest from the days before the Law[63] who was unconnected to Israel.

In heaven the Lord Jesus maintains a priestly work for us and we still praise and pray through Him or "in His Name" in the same way that the worshipper depended on the work of a priest. His heavenly ministry removes the need for an earthly sanctuary. If there is now only one priest, the great high priest of Hebrews, there is also ironically a massive expansion of the priesthood. Luther dubbed this truth "the priesthood of all believers" thus rejecting the teaching of the Roman Catholic church that interposes priests between the people and God. In the N.T. every Christian now has the privilege of offering the "sacrifice of praise" – he does not need a Levite. Every Christian is a priest. The priesthood of believers does not mean there is no need of a priest for believers – that work is continued by Christ.

---

[63] Gen. 14:18.

KEY SCRIPTURES

¹ And take thou unto thee Aaron thy brother, and his sons with him, from among the children of Israel, that he may minister unto me in the priest's office, *even* Aaron, Nadab and Abihu, Eleazar and Ithamar, Aaron's sons. ² And thou shalt make holy garments for Aaron thy brother for glory and for beauty.

Ex. 28:1-2

⁴ And Aaron and his sons thou shalt bring unto the door of the tabernacle of the congregation, and shalt wash them with water. ⁵ And thou shalt take the garments, and put upon Aaron the coat, and the robe of the ephod, and the ephod, and the breastplate, and gird him with the curious girdle of the ephod: ⁶ And thou shalt put the mitre upon his head, and put the holy crown upon the mitre. ⁷ Then shalt thou take the anointing oil, and pour *it* upon his head, and anoint him. ⁸ And thou shalt bring his sons, and put coats upon them. ⁹ And thou shalt gird them with girdles, Aaron and his sons, and put the bonnets on them: and the priest's office shall be theirs for a perpetual statute: and thou shalt consecrate Aaron and his sons.

Ex. 29:4-9

¹ For every high priest taken from among men is ordained for men in things *pertaining* to God, that he may offer both gifts and sacrifices for sins: ² Who can have compassion on the ignorant, and on them that are out of the way; for that he himself also is compassed with infirmity. ³ And by reason hereof he ought, as for the people, so also for himself, to offer for sins. ⁴ And no man taketh this honour unto himself, but he that is called of God, as *was* Aaron. ⁵ So also Christ glorified not himself to be made an high priest; but he that said unto him, Thou art my Son, to day have I begotten thee. ⁶ As he saith also in another *place*, Thou *art* a priest for ever after the order of Melchisedec.

Heb. 5:1-6

[11] And every priest standeth daily ministering and offering oftentimes the same sacrifices, which can never take away sins: [12] But this man, after he had offered one sacrifice for sins for ever, sat down on the right hand of God;

Heb. 10:11-12

[5] Ye also, as lively stones, are built up a spiritual house, an holy priesthood, to offer up spiritual sacrifices, acceptable to God by Jesus Christ.... [9] But ye *are* a chosen generation, a royal priesthood, an holy nation, a peculiar people; that ye should shew forth the praises of him who hath called you out of darkness into his marvellous light:

1 Pet. 2:5, 9

KEY QUOTES

The quality of the whole of these vestments, whether it was texture or material or workmanship, was the very best of its kind – fine linen, pure gold, precious stones, costly ointment, cunning workmanship.... This was because it was all a type of Christ's character, and nothing but the highest quality will do to portray Him.[64]

CW Slemming

The biblical doctrine of the priesthood of all believers (1 Peter 2:9; Rev. 1:6) eliminates the need to go through intermediaries—such as Mary, the saints, or human priests—to obtain access to the Father. The great Reformer Martin Luther assaulted the Roman counterfeit when he wrote, "It says in 1 Peter 2:9, 'Ye are an elect race, a royal priesthood, and a priestly kingdom.' It follows that all of us who are Christians are also priests" ("The Pagan Servitude of the Church," *Martin Luther: Selections from His Writings* p. 345). That Christians have direct priestly access to the Father does not, however, obviate the need for Christ's intercession on their behalf as their Great High Priest (Isa. 53:12; Rom. 8:34; Heb. 7:25; cf. 1 John 2:1-2).[65]

John MacArthur

---

[64] These are the Garments (CLC) p. 27.
[65] MacArthur New Testament Commentary – John 12-21, p. 226.

KEY QUESTIONS

1. Why did God not allow any man to be a priest in the Tabernacle?

2. What family supplied the priests for the Tabernacle?

3. In the N.T. what scriptures teach that all believers are priests?

4. Is the Lord Jesus a priest from Aaron's line?

The Anointing Oil

Key Points

- Aromatic oil was used to sanctify persons and objects in the Tabernacle.

- Oil in scripture is typical of the Holy Spirit.

- Sweet spices in scripture are typical of the attractiveness of Christ.

- The meaning of "Messiah" is the "anointed one".

The Choice of the Anointing Oil

"Anointing oil" was an aromatic liquid made of olive oil. It was reserved for the use of the priesthood and Tabernacle. It took its name from its method of application. "Anointing" literally means to "smear".[66] The oil was applied to the head of the priest[67] and on the vessels[68] of the Tabernacle. The act of anointing was designed to mark God's approval and the consecration of the person or object to God.

Ordinary oil was used for the body[69] and face[70] to keep skin smooth and supple. It was also used to soothe irritation or inflammation.[71] At times ordinary oil was used for symbolic

---

[66] *Mashach*. As a liquid it could be applied with the finger and poured out; see e.g. Lev. 8:12.
[67] Ps. 133:2; althogh all priests were anointed (Ex. 28:41; 30:30; Num. 3:3) it seems that the expression "the priest that is anointed" (Lev. 4:3, 5, 16) refers to the High Priest (Lev. 21:10). His anointing seems to have been somewhat different; see Lev. 8:12 where he is anointed personally. The whole priesthood is subsequently anointed (Lev. 8:30).
[68] Ex. 29:36 – the altar of burnt offering; 30:26 - the ark; 40:11 – the laver. Ex. 40:9 indicates that all the vessels were anointed.
[69] Ruth 3:3; 2 Sam. 12:20.
[70] Ps. 104:15.
[71] Is. 1:6; Lk. 10:34.

purposes. Kings were anointed with oil.[72] There is also an indication that prophets were anointed.[73]

There were three liquids associated with the Tabernacle - blood, water and oil. They are handled is distinct ways. Blood is sprinkled or poured. Water is for bathing. Oil is used to anoint. Psalm 133 describes Moses anointing of Aaron. The oil runs down to the skirt of his garment which would suggest copious quantities were used. While blood and water were in constant use in the Tabernacle anointing oil was used infrequently.

The Composition of the Anointing Oil

Anointing oil was made of a variety of fragrant ingredients most of which remain in use today. But whereas today perfume is usually in liquid form, these fragrances were based in oil. That oil was derived from the crushing of olives. Oil itself was used for everyday purposes such as cooking[74] and fuelling lamps[75] as well as the medicinal and cosmetic purposes we have noted.[76]

The chief spices were myrrh and cassia. 500 shekels of myrrh and 500 shekels of cassia were prescribed for per batch. One shekel is 0.4 of an ounce or 11.6 grams.[77] Lesser quantities, 250 shekels, were prescribed for cinnamon and calamus. Since these spices were traded in solid form it follows that they would have to be ground or strained in order to be suitable to mix with oil[78] and thus to create a liquid. If spices weighing 1500 shekels (17.3 kg or 38 lbs) are mixed with one hin of oil (8 pints) this would create a large quantity of oil that was thereafter used as necessity arose. It would therefore seem that these measurements describe the weights required when a batch or store of oil was made. Lesser or greater quantities (even if in the same proportions) were not permitted.

The Creation of the Anointing Oil

The "art" or skill of blending aromatic spices was that of the apothecary. The

---

[72] Saul – 1 Sam. 10:1; David – 1 Sam 16:3; Solomon – 1 Kings 1:39.
[73] 1 Kings 19:15-16.
[74] 1 Kings 17:12.
[75] Matt. 25:3.
[76] Eccl. 9:8.
[77] Logos Weights and Measures converter.
[78] Myrrh is a resin obtained by cutting tree bark of commiphora myrrha. It solidifies into hard crystals and was traded in this form. Cassia and cinnamon are aromatic oils from the bark of a tree. Calamus is thought to be a form of sweet cane, though this identification is not certain.

apothecary in O.T. times was a perfumer. To make spices he not only used locally obtained ingredients but also those from farther afield. Myrrh in biblical times came from Arabia, Ethiopia and India. Cassia was probably imported from India. Cinnamon originated in China though it was transplanted to Eastern lands. The apothecaries did not supply the Tabernacle or Temple. The task of making anointing oil and incense for the censers was for the priests. Making a blend of the same spices for other uses was forbidden under pain of death.[79] No doubt these spices were used in other aromatic oils but the priests were not permitted to make this particular blend and sell it for profane purposes. It was reserved to the Tabernacle.

The four spices in the anointing oil are paralleled with four spices used in the incense. They were frankincense[80] stacte[81] onycha[82] and galbanum.[83] They too were solids that were ground before being mixed to make the incense.

The Character of the Anointing Oil

Oil is along with blood and water one of the three main liquids associated with the Tabernacle. Blood was a means of atonement and water was a cleansing agent. Oil principally spoke of God's power as mediated through the Spirit. The power of oil in the natural realm was to create light and warmth. In the spiritual realm it signified parallel benefits. The oil represented God's ability to bring understanding and wisdom to the affairs of life. It also signified the power that God through the Spirit provided for His service. Where the oil was mixed with spices the idea of fragrance or beauty is added to these features. As with incense the attractiveness is not seen or heard but smelled. Fragrance can be appreciated even in darkness. The spiritual lesson here is that God's help and blessing can be known whatever the conditions. Fragrance also lingers. Music may be beautiful but once the final note has died away it has gone. The fragrance of anointing oil by contrast lingered long after it had been poured out.

Incense required a flame in order to release its odour whereas anointing oil

---

[79] "Cut off" usually means death by stoning but may also mean excommunication or ostracizing people or groups of people (Deut. 19:1). In the N.T. it does not signify capital punishment e.g. Rom. 9:3; 11:22. This penalty was prescribed for Sabbath breaking (Ex. 30; 33, 38; 31:14; cf. 12:15, 19).
[80] Levonah.
[81] Nataph.
[82] Shecheleth.
[83] Chelbinah.

required only to be poured from its horn or bottle. Incense rose up whereas oil flowed down. Thus although incense and anointing oil were both fragrant they functioned in different ways.

The Tabernacle is a "feast" for the senses. Its fabrics are made of a variety of colours, golden bells chime on the High Priest's garments and incense and anointing oil waft sweet smells through the air. The Tabernacle speaks of the Messiah[84] (lit. "the anointed One"). He was anointed in the offices of Prophet, Priest and King. As prophet He was anointed to preach the gospel (Lk. 4:18), as priest He was anointed with the oil of gladness (Heb. 1:9) and as King of Israel he was "the Lord's anointed" (Acts 4:27; Ps 2:2). As spices brought the fragrance of other lands to the wilderness so Christ brought something of heaven into this world.

[84] *Mashiach.*

 **KEY QUOTES**

In the Old Testament, when Aaron and his sons were presented for priestly service (Ex 29), there were sacrifices killed, and blood was shed and applied before the oil, but there was no mention of sacrifices or blood applied to this blessed Man before the Holy Spirit came upon Christ in Luke 3.21,22. There was no need for blood or bathing to take place first. The Spirit had come upon men and then departed, but He alighted on Christ and abode. Jesus will later be seen as the man approved of God by miracles, signs, and wonders. Here, however, He was commencing His public ministry anointed of the Holy Spirit without water or blood, no need for sin to be atoned for, no need for defilement to be cleansed, no need for a mediator to take up His cause.[85]

Jimmy Paton

....the people in the midst of whom God will dwell will be a *powerful people*, a people in the good of the anointing, allowing the Spirit of God to control. In the New Testament three times over the word "anoint" is used concerning believers, and it has to do with the Spirit of God (2 Cor 1.21; James 5.14; 1 Jn 2.20, as "unction").[86]

Phil Harding

[85] Jimmy Paton "The Offerings" Believers Magazine (December 2005).
[86] Phil Harding "Musings from Exodus" Believers Magazine (September 2013).

KEY QUESTIONS

1. What was the purpose of anointing the priests with oil?

2. Why were spices added to the oil?

3. Why is oil a suitable emblem of the Spirit?

4. What were the purposes of blood, water and oil in the Tabernacle?

The Offerings

Key Points

- There are three sweet savour offerings (the burnt offering, the meal offering and the peace offering) and two non-sweet savour offerings (the sin offering and trespass offering).

- The burnt offering is the foundational offering of the Levitical system and was given, with minor exceptions, in its entirety to God.

- The meal offering is, with one exception, the only bloodless offering in the Levitical offerings.

- The trespass offering was required where the wrongful act for which it was offered had caused loss or damage to someone's property.

The Purpose of Offerings

Before the Tabernacle was built those who worshipped God or who sought to express their submission to Him offered sacrifices. The usual way of doing so was to build an altar of stone and burn a sacrifice on the altar. The symbolism behind this was that the flames transformed the sacrifice and sent it upwards to God in the form of smoke. The worshipper thus "gave" to God something that was valuable to him such as a lamb or bull. This giving represented two basic ideas. First it was a form of worship. As we give gifts to those whom we love or respect so they gave to God an offering. Second it was given as a substitute. The blood represented the life of the offering. It was poured out or sprinkled at the altar. The offeror thus recognised that his sins deserved death but the sacrifice had taken his place. The bull or lamb was his substitute.

The Practice of Offering

The first offerings mentioned in scripture were those of Cain and Abel.[87] The Patriarchs all offered sacrifices. There is little guidance given in Genesis about how the Patriarchs knew what to offer or how to offer. The terminology of "offering" and "sacrifice" reveals that they understood that it was a form of worship. The word "offering" means a gift or present.[88] They also understood that they were substitutionary. The word "sacrifice" means death or slaughter.[89] The books of Genesis and Exodus refer to burnt offerings[90] and meat offerings.[91] It was only once Israel reached Sinai that the peace offering,[92] sin offering[93] and trespass[94] offering appear.

The Principal Offerings

The five Levitical offerings are –
- The Burnt Offering
- The Meat offering
- The Peace Offering
- The Sin Offering
- The Trespass Offering

The Burnt Offering - The words "burnt offering" translate a single Hebrew word olah which means "ascending offering". Leviticus lays down rules for the burnt offering. Some of the principles were already familiar. Leviticus required clean animals to be offered. The idea that some animals were clean however went back to the days of Noah.[95] Some of the rules may have been statements of existing practice e.g. the animal had to be unblemished and a male. But some of the rules were almost certainly new e.g. that the whole animal should be burned on the altar. The burnt offering is the quintessential offering.   In its pre-Levitical form it was the first to be offered. In the Leviticus offerings it is the first in the list. It is the most common form of offering. They were offered for individuals

---

[87] Gen. 4:3, 4.
[88] Minchah.
[89] Zebach.
[90] Noah (Gen. 8:20) offered the first "burnt offering". Isaac was to be a "burnt offering" (Gen. 22:2, 8).
[91] The word minchah appears in Gen. 4:3; Ex 29:41.
[92] Ex. 20:24.
[93] The only reference to a sin offering as such is Ex. 29:14, though the word chattah is used in Genesis to mean sin although not an offering for sin.
[94] Lev. 5:6.
[95] Gen. 7:2.

as and when required and also in obedience to the Law at the prescribed daily offerings[96] and set feasts.

Meat Offering - The "meat offering" translates the Hebrew word *minchah* which means "a gift". Before Leviticus gift offerings were used in a wide sense to cover all offerings. But in Leviticus the offering is confined to bloodless offerings of flour, cakes or ears of corn. Unlike the burnt offering these offerings were not burnt in their entirety on the altar but handfuls were burnt on the altar. This handful was called the memorial. The remainder was used to provide food for the priests. The offering was accompanied by frankincense which emphasised the idea that the offering had a sweet smell to God. They were also accompanied by oil which speaks of the Holy Spirit.

Peace Offering - Peace offerings are not mentioned in Genesis or in the early chapters of Exodus. The first reference is after Israel reached Sinai.[97] This may mean that they were not in use until the Law was given.[98] "Peace offering" translates the Hebrew word *selem* which means peace or satisfaction. This carries the idea not only that God is contented with the offering but also the offeror is contented as well. He brings the offering out of a sense of wellbeing or contentment. The fat on various specified parts of the animal was reserved for God and burnt on the altar. The remainder could be eaten by the friends and family of the offeror.

Sin and Trespass Offerings - The sin and trespass offerings are not expressions of worship in the same way as the burnt, meat and peace offerings. They focus on atonement for sin. Thus although the first three offerings are described as "sweet savour offerings" there is no such description attached to the sin and trespass offerings.[99] The simple reason for this is that there is nothing pleasant about sin. The sin offering was not actually available for sin in general. It was for sins of "ignorance". Ignorance covers sins committed in weakness or carelessness. It was not available for deliberate or "high handed" sins. The lack of an offering for deliberate sin and for man's sinful nature demonstrates the incomplete nature

[96] Ex. 29:38.
[97] Ex. 20:24.
[98] The opening chapters of Leviticus where the Law of the Offerings is set out run on directly from the end of the book of Exodus.
[99] Lev. 4:31 is the exception.

of the O.T. offerings. Unlike the other offerings the sin offering was burnt in two locations. Part on the altar and part outside the Camp.

The type of offering required varied according to the responsibility of the sinner and the means of the offeror. Thus if the High Priest sinned ("the priest that is anointed") he had to bring a large offering because he should have known better. On the other hand if a poor man sinned he was able to bring a small offering.

The sin offering and trespass offering are very similar in many ways. The distinguishing feature of the trespass offering was that it involved payment of money. This may have meant that it was used when the trespass involved someone suffering loss. So for example if someone borrowed an animal and through his fault it was injured while in his custody, he would have to offer a trespass offering as well as compensation to the owner. It seems that Moses[100] or perhaps the priest valued the damage done. The tariff for the offeror was compensation for the loss plus 20%.[101] The 20% was paid to the to the owner if the damage was done to private property. If the damage was done to the "holy things" e.g. the Tabernacle furniture or vessels the value of the damage plus 20% was paid to the priest. The money was no doubt used for the Tabernacle.

The Promise of the Offerings
The sweet savour offerings anticipate the Lord Jesus' offering of Himself on Calvary. They show that although the death of Christ was a fearsome experience for the Lord Jesus His offering brought pleasure to the heart of God. The sin offering emphasised the idea that the Lord Jesus would put away sin by the sacrifice of Himself.

---

[100] Lev. 5:14.
[101] Lev. 6:5.

KEY SCRIPTURES

² Speak unto the children of Israel, and say unto them, If any man of you bring an offering unto the LORD, ye shall bring your offering of the cattle, *even* of the herd, and of the flock. ³ If his offering *be* a burnt sacrifice of the herd, let him offer a male without blemish: he shall offer it of his own voluntary will at the door of the tabernacle of the congregation before the LORD. ⁴ And he shall put his hand upon the head of the burnt offering; and it shall be accepted for him to make atonement for him.

Lev. 1:2-4

¹ And when any will offer a meat offering unto the LORD, his offering shall be *of* fine flour; and he shall pour oil upon it, and put frankincense thereon: ² And he shall bring it to Aaron's sons the priests: and he shall take thereout his handful of the flour thereof, and of the oil thereof, with all the frankincense thereof; and the priest shall burn the memorial of it upon the altar, *to be* an offering made by fire, of a sweet savour unto the LORD:

Lev. 2:1-2

¹ And if his oblation *be* a sacrifice of peace offering, if he offer *it* of the herd; whether *it be* a male or female, he shall offer it without blemish before the LORD. ² And he shall lay his hand upon the head of his offering, and kill it *at* the door of the tabernacle of the congregation: and Aaron's sons the priests shall sprinkle the blood upon the altar round about. ³ And he shall offer of the sacrifice of the peace offering an offering made by fire unto the LORD; the fat that covereth the inwards, and all the fat that *is* upon the inwards, ⁴ And the two kidneys, and the fat that *is* on them, which *is* by the flanks, and the caul above the liver, with the kidneys, it shall he take away. ⁵ And Aaron's sons shall burn it on the altar upon the burnt sacrifice, which *is* upon the wood that *is* on the fire: *it is* an offering made by fire, of a sweet savour unto the LORD.

Lev. 3:1-5

KEY SCRIPTURES

¹ And the LORD spake unto Moses, saying, ² Speak unto the children of Israel, saying, If a soul shall sin through ignorance against any of the commandments of the LORD *concerning things* which ought not to be done, and shall do against any of them: ³ If the priest that is anointed do sin according to the sin of the people; then let him bring for his sin, which he hath sinned, a young bullock without blemish unto the LORD for a sin offering.

Lev. 4:1-3

¹³ And if the whole congregation of Israel sin through ignorance, and the thing be hid from the eyes of the assembly, and they have done *somewhat against* any of the commandments of the LORD *concerning things* which should not be done, and are guilty; ¹⁴When the sin, which they have sinned against it, is known, then the congregation shall offer a young bullock for the sin, and bring him before the tabernacle of the congregation. ¹⁵ And the elders of the congregation shall lay their hands upon the head of the bullock before the LORD: and the bullock shall be killed before the LORD.

Lev. 4:13-15

²² When a ruler hath sinned, and done *somewhat* through ignorance *against* any of the commandments of the LORD his God *concerning things* which should not be done, and is guilty; ²³ Or if his sin, wherein he hath sinned, come to his knowledge; he shall bring his offering, a kid of the goats, a male without blemish:... ²⁷ And if any one of the common people sin through ignorance, while he doeth *somewhat against* any of the commandments of the LORD *concerning things* which ought not to be done, and be guilty; ²⁸ Or if his sin, which he hath sinned, come to his knowledge: then he shall bring his offering, a kid of the goats, a female without blemish, for his sin which he hath sinned.

Lev. 4:22-23; 27-28

KEY SCRIPTURES

² And walk in love, as Christ also hath loved us, and hath given himself for us an offering and a sacrifice to Lord for a sweet smelling savour.

Eph. 5:2

¹⁸ But I have all, and abound: I am full, having received of Epaphroditus the things which were sent from you, an odour of a sweet smell, a sacrifice acceptable, well pleasing to God.

Phil. 4:18

KEY QUOTES

The offerings portray the glory of Christ's person, the beauty of His character and the greatness of His work. They show His people His inestimable preciousness to God both in the loveliness of His life and in the value of His sacrifice; and they describe in detail the privilege of believers of approach to God in the holy exercises of supplication and worship[102]

Jim Flanigan

1 – Man is a guilty transgressor and needs forgiveness – Leviticus ch 5 The Trespass Offering.

2 – He is a sinner and needs an atoning sacrifice – Leviticus ch 4 The Sin Offering.

3 – He is in heart alienated from God and needs reconciliation – Leviticus ch 3 The Peace Offering.

4 - He is fallen and depraved in nature and needs as a substitute One who is harmless, undefiled and separate from sinners – Leviticus ch 2 The Meat Offering.

5 – He is utterly unworthy in himself, without anything of his own to recommend him to God; he needs therefore to be identified with God who is altogether worthy and an object of divine favour that he might be accepted in God's Beloved – Leviticus ch 1 The Burnt or Ascending Offering.[103]

Thomas Newberry

---

[02] Christ in the Levitical offerings (John Ritchie) p. 8.
[03] Types of Levitical offerings (John Ritchie) p. 10.

KEY QUESTIONS

1. What is the key characteristic of the Burnt Offering?

2. What is the key characteristic of the Meal Offering?

3. What is the difference between the sin and trespass offering?

4. Which offering also provided food for the offeror?